GIFTS
FROM THE
KITCHEN

BARBARA RANDOLPH

Doubleday Canada Limited, Toronto

A FRIEDMAN GROUP BOOK

Copyright © 1991 by Michael Friedman Publishing Group, Inc.

First published in Canada in 1991 by Doubleday Canada Limited.

Canadian Cataloguing-in-Publication Data

Randolph, Barbara
Gifts from the kitchen

Includes index.
ISBN 0-385-25332-X

1. Cookery. 2. Handicraft. 3. Gifts.
I. Title.

TX714.R63 1991   641.5   C91-093786-9

GIFTS FROM THE KITCHEN
was prepared and produced by
Michael Friedman Publishing Group, Inc.
15 West 26th Street
New York, New York 10010

Editor: Sharon Kalman
Designer: Lynne Yeamans
Photography Editor: Anne K. Price

Typeset by Bookworks Plus
Color separation by Excel Graphic Arts Ltd.
Printed and bound in Hong Kong by Leefung-Asco Printers Ltd.

Published in Canada by
Doubleday Canada Limited
105 Bond Street
Toronto, Ontario
M5B 1Y3

Kitchen Metrics

Spoons

¼ teaspoon	= 1 milliliter
½ teaspoon	= 2 milliliters
1 teaspoon	= 5 milliliters
1 tablespoon	= 15 milliliters
2 tablespoons	= 25 milliliters
3 tablespoons	= 50 milliliters

Cups

¼ cup	= 50 milliliters
⅓ cup	= 75 milliliters
½ cup	= 125 milliliters
⅔ cup	= 150 milliliters
¾ cup	= 175 milliliters
1 cup	= 250 milliliters

Oven Temperatures

200°F	= 100°C	350°F	= 180°C
225°F	= 110°C	375°F	= 190°C
250°F	= 120°C	400°F	= 200°C
275°F	= 140°C	425°F	= 220°C
300°F	= 150°C	450°F	= 230°C
325°F	= 160°C	475°F	= 240°C

© Michael Skott

CONTENTS
❧

Introduction

While any handmade present is a gift of love, those from the kitchen are straight from the heart. Taking the time and effort to create a special dish, bake a loaf of bread, or preserve the fruits of the local harvest says that you care in a way that few gifts can match.

Baking or preserving can fit into even the busiest schedule. It is just as easy to bake four loaves of a favorite fruit or yeast bread as it is to bake one or two loaves. Recipes for jams, jellies, and pickles nearly always make at least several jars. By setting aside one day or evening to make preserves, you can avoid having to get out all the equipment and ingredients more than once. While you are waiting for a batch of jam to thicken, you have time to make a few jars of pickles.

The same is true of baking. While you are waiting for bread to rise or to bake, the flour and other ingredients are handy to make a few sheets of cookies. Some of the recipes in this book can be made well in advance, others can be kept a few days until you are ready to present them. Each is designed to create a beautiful gift that will enrich your own enjoyment of the holiday season as well.

PRESENTING YOUR GIFTS FROM THE KITCHEN

Half the fun of giving foods is in thinking up interesting ways to wrap and present them. Most foods look festive enough to be given as they are, perhaps with only a bow and a tag added. Since perishable gifts should be used or refrigerated as they arrive, a label is also a way to let the recipient know that the gift is for immediate use.

To create a larger gift, assemble a collection of homemade goodies into a basket or other appropriate container. You can mix your own foods with fresh apples, giant grapefruit, or other fruit, and decorate the basket with sprigs of fresh greens.

Food baskets are more fun to assemble and package if they have a theme, such as teatime or Italian foods. The theme you choose often suggests packaging and other small nonfood items to include with the products of your own kitchen. Choose a theme that will suit the lifestyle of the person to whom you are giving the gift.

A student away at school will always appreciate a gift of snack foods that keep well. These should be ready-to-eat foods, such as cookies, small loaves of bread, and packets of tea and hot cocoa mix. Package these in a tin box with a tight-fitting lid and include a coffee mug and tea infuser.

A friend who entertains a lot would appreciate a crock of cheese presented on a wooden cheese board with packets of hot-mulled-cider spices. Present a tray of cookies arranged ready for serving, or candy in a glass candy dish. Give a loaf of bread atop a wooden bread board, a bright ribbon tied around both. Fill a china cup with your own tea blends and tie an infuser to the handle with ribbon. Package hot cocoa mix in a pottery mug.

Long, narrow, rectangular baskets meant for serving crackers make perfect holders for jars of jams, jellies, or pickles. Line them up in a row inside and wrap the whole basket.

Oval Shaker-style boxes can be decorated with stenciled designs and filled with packets of herbs and tea blends. Larger ones can hold a small loaf of tea bread.

Friends who share your concern for the environment will appreciate having gifts arrive in reusable calico gift bags (see instructions on page 13). These have the advantage of concealing the contents quickly and easily, no matter how odd the shape or how hard to wrap. Jars of pre-serves, vinegars, or mustards, packages of homemade pasta, even loaves of bread are easy to wrap in bags. These are especially useful for wrapping food gifts that are to be mailed, since the fabric does not rip or wrinkle like paper wrapping.

© Michael Skott

PACKING FOODS TO SHIP

There are a few tricks that make it easy to ship even those foods that are in jars and bottles. The first thing to remember is that objects packed snugly are safer than those with room to move. The second is to double-box everything. By combining these two principles and using enough soft material to cushion breakables, gifts will arrive safe and delicious every time.

Environmentally conscious packers are shunning the polystyrene packing "peanuts" and using popcorn instead. Pop it without oil and use it to cushion fragile items. To package jars, roll each in recycled porous paper such as grocery bags, which do not leave ink on your wrappings as newspaper would. Pack them in a box just large enough to hold them snugly, then set that box, sealed shut with tape, into a larger carton, with a layer of popcorn in the bottom. Surround the smaller box with popcorn and cover the top with another layer of popcorn. Close the larger carton and shake it to make sure the inside box cannot shift about.

Remember when mailing jams and preserves to certain destinations, that the packages may be stored at temperatures below freezing. Your packing will help insulate, but it is best to label these packages "Do not freeze." Your post office or private shipper can be very helpful in suggesting safe packing and shipping techniques for perishable items.

If sending packages to warmer climates, it is best not to send anything containing chocolate, since it is likely to melt before it reaches its final destination.

CALICO GIFT BAGS

Cut a piece of fabric twice the size necessary for the finished bag. Fold in half with the right sides facing and stitch along two sides to form a bag. Trim the open edge with pinking scissors and turn to the right side. Press the bag to smooth the seams and stitch a narrow ribbon to one side-seam so that its center is secured a few inches below the top of the bag.

Make these in sizes to fit bottles and jars, taking care to allow for the thickness as well as the width of the jar when measuring the size.

Christmas print fabrics are plentiful before the holidays, but any bright fabric will do. Ginghams and stripes are particularly suited to food gifts. Unbleached muslin makes homey bags with a natural air. Use earth tones and deep colors for the ribbons or tie them with bows of jute twine. Stencil simple designs on the muslin bags for a country touch.

© Steven Mark Needham/Envision

Chapter One

Fresh from the Oven

Nothing brings the essence of the holiday season into your home as quickly as a batch of spicy cookies or bread in the oven. These rich fragrances waft into every corner of the house and bring everyone running to the kitchen.

While you needn't set up an industrial-sized assembly line to make a few batches of cookies, there are a few tricks that will make the job go faster and easier. Line cookie sheets with foil. While one batch is baking, fill another sheet of foil with cookies to be baked. When the first cookies come out of the oven, simply slide the foil sheets off, replace them with the unbaked ones, and return the cookie sheet to the oven. This not only uses your oven more efficiently, but it saves time (and you don't have to wash the cookie sheets after each batch). Slide the foil with baked cookies right onto a rack and allow cookies to set before peeling them off.

Make several kinds of cookies and present mixed boxes or tins. Bake fruit breads in small loaf pans and give two different ones. These are especially nice for someone who lives alone, since they can put the second loaf in the refrigerator or freezer. Small loaves will also ship better than larger ones.

HOLIDAY SHORTBREAD

A Scottish favorite all year-round, these tender, buttery cookies are a fine gift by themselves or may be baked in smaller sizes to combine with an assortment of other cookies and sweets.

1 ¼ cups plus 2 tablespoons butter at
*   room temperature*
¾ cup sugar
¼ teaspoon salt
3 ½ cups flour

Cream the butter with sugar and salt and beat until fluffy. Work in flour, wrap dough in waxed paper, and refrigerate one hour.

Roll dough on a lightly floured surface to ¼ inch thick and cut into 5-inch circles, using a cookie cutter with a fluted edge.

Move carefully to lightly buttered cookie sheets and prick with a fork to divide each cookie into four wedges. Do not break the cookie apart, simply make two crossed rows of perforations. Bake about 20 minutes or until they are golden brown at the edges. Remove from the oven and sprinkle lightly with sugar while they are still hot. When they have cooled slightly, remove the cookies to a baking rack. Store in a tightly sealed container, where they will keep for several weeks.

Makes approximately 1 ½ dozen
cookies.

© Steven Mark Needham/Envision

© Tony Cenicola

Gingerbread People

Gingerbread cookies are a good project for children because the dough is not sticky or difficult to handle.

½ cup molasses
¼ cup sugar
3 tablespoons butter or shortening
1 tablespoon milk
2 cups flour
½ teaspoon baking soda
½ teaspoon salt
¼ teaspoon nutmeg
1 teaspoon ginger
¼ teaspoon cloves
½ teaspoon cinnamon
Currants (or raisins) for decoration

Heat molasses just to boiling and add sugar, butter, and milk. Sift together flour, baking soda, salt, nutmeg, ginger, cloves, and cinnamon and stir into molasses mixture, adding more flour if necessary to make dough stiff enough to roll. Using one small piece of dough at a time, roll to just under ¼ inch thick and cut gingerbread people. To decorate before baking, use currants or raisins for faces and buttons. Bake at 375°F until cookies begin to darken on the bottom. It may help to keep the unused dough in the refrigerator while each batch is being rolled out.

Makes enough to fill 2 cookie sheets.

COTTAGE COOKIES

These delicious cookies are served at The King's Cottage, an elegant bed and breakfast in Lancaster, Pennsylvania. Each year at Christmas a group of fine Lancaster inns joins in hosting a tour so visitors can see the beautiful holiday decorations in each. The King's Cottage welcomes its guests with these cookies. Since they are cut into neat squares, they pack very well in candy boxes.

½ cup butter

½ cup sugar

2 egg yolks

1 teaspoon vanilla

1½ cups sifted flour

1 teaspoon baking powder

½ teaspoon salt

Topping:

2 egg whites

1 cup brown sugar

1 cup chopped nuts (optional)

Cream butter and sugar; add egg yolks. Mix remaining batter ingredients well. Spread in an ungreased 8 x 8-inch pan.

Beat egg whites until stiff and add brown sugar (and nuts, if you're using them). Pour topping over the dough in the pan. Bake at 325°F for 45 minutes. When cool, cut in bars.

Makes about 2 dozen.

BLUEBERRY-ORANGE MUFFINS

If you can't bake these tempting muffins and deliver them hot at teatime, don't despair. They freeze well, maintaining both their flavor and texture. Attach a tag suggesting that they be warmed briefly in a moderate oven before serving.

¼ cup butter
¼ cup sugar
1 beaten egg
2 cups flour
4 teaspoons baking powder
½ teaspoon salt
½ teaspoon nutmeg
1 cup milk
2 cups blueberries
Grated outer peel of one orange

Cream butter and sugar, add beaten egg, and mix well. Sift in the dry ingredients alternately with milk, mixing well. Do not beat; the batter should be lumpy. Fold in berries and orange peel and spoon batter into greased muffin tins, filling only half full. Bake at 375°F for 30 minutes or until evenly browned.

Makes 18 muffins.

APPLE-CRANBERRY MUFFINS

Dried cranberries are available in gourmet stores, but if you cannot find them, substitute fresh ones, coarsely chopped and drained. Like the Blueberry-Orange Muffins, these freeze well and can be warmed in the oven just prior to serving.

2 cups sifted flour
½ cup sugar
¾ teaspoon salt
1 tablespoon baking powder
1 teaspoon cinnamon
½ teaspoon nutmeg
1 egg, well beaten
1¼ cups milk
¼ cup melted shortening
1½ teaspoons lemon juice
1¼ cups finely chopped apples
½ cup dried cranberries

Sift together flour, sugar, salt, baking powder, cinnamon, and nutmeg; combine egg, milk, and shortening. Add liquids to dry ingredients and stir barely enough to mix. Pour lemon juice over apples and stir into batter with the cranberries. Do not overmix. Fill greased muffin tins two-thirds full and bake at 425°F for 25 minutes.

Makes 16 muffins.

HANCOCK INN PUMPKIN BREAD

The Hancock Inn in Hancock, New Hampshire, serves its guests this rich, delicious bread.

1 cup brown sugar
1 cup white sugar
1 cup oil
3 eggs
2 to 3 cups mashed pumpkin
1 cup chopped nuts
1 cup raisins
3 cups flour
1½ teaspoons cloves
1½ teaspoons cinnamon
½ teaspoon allspice
1½ teaspoons nutmeg
½ teaspoon baking powder
1 teaspoon baking soda
½ teaspoon salt

Mix sugars and oil. Add eggs, mashed pumpkin, nuts, and raisins. Sift together flour, cloves, cinnamon, allspice, nutmeg, baking powder, baking soda, and salt, and add. Bake in greased loaf pans at 350°F for 1 to 1½ hours until it is brown and tests done in the middle.

Makes 2 large or 4 small loaves.

© Glenn David Smith

WHITE BREAD

Nothing could be more homey or more simple than a loaf of white yeast bread fresh from the oven. But few gifts are received with as much enthusiasm as is home-baked white bread. Bread is symbolic of hearth, home, and hospitality, so there can be no better way to share your home with friends than with a loaf of your own baking. Package it proudly in a clear bag with a brightly colored ribbon tied around its plump middle.

¾ cup sugar

4 teaspoons salt

¼ cup vegetable oil

4 cups milk, lukewarm

2 packages dry yeast, dissolved in ½
   cup lukewarm water

12 cups flour

Combine sugar, salt, and oil with milk and add yeast. Stir in flour a cup at a time until the dough is stiff. Turn dough out onto a well-floured board and knead 15 minutes, adding remaining flour to the board as necessary.

Place in a large, greased bowl, cover with a towel, and let rise in a warm place until doubled. Punch down with a floured fist and let rise again. Punch down, divide into fourths, and shape into loaves. Place these in greased loaf pans and let rise again. Bake in a 350°F oven for 45 minutes or until bread feels crisp and hollow when tapped with the finger. During the baking, move loaves around once to make sure they all bake evenly.

Makes 4 loaves, but is easily cut in half.

DOG BONES

Hearty, healthy, homemade treats for the family dog can be given as a separate gift or included in a goody basket for the whole family. Be sure to label them with the dog's name or the owner might mistake them for people cookies!

1 cup white flour
1 cup whole wheat flour
½ cup wheat germ
½ teaspoon salt
1 teaspoon brewers' yeast
6 tablespoons chilled bacon drippings
½ cup dry milk
1 egg
½ cup water

Mix flours, wheat germ, salt, yeast, and dry milk and cut in fat as you would for pie crust. Beat egg and stir into this mixture. Add water, stirring, only until you can gather this into a stiff dough. Knead 2 to 3 minutes until smooth and roll to ½ inch thick. Cut with a bone-shaped cookie cutter. Bake on greased cookie sheet at 325°F for about 25 minutes or until brown.

Makes approximately 12 to 16 bones.

Chapter Two

From the Preserving Kettle

Crystal shimmering jellies and bright translucent pickles are among the loveliest and most treasured gifts. And for the busy cook, they are a blessing, since they can be prepared weeks or months ahead.

Pack pickles and fruits evenly—all pieces the same size and rows of pickle slices set flat against the edge of the jar in even rows. Jellies look their best if they are perfectly clear, so let juice strain overnight and pour off the top juice leaving any sediment on the bottom.

Store jars in a cool place without their metal rings until you are ready to wrap them for gifts. A day or two before, bring jars from storage and let them adjust to room temperature. Quickly dip each jar into barely simmering water to which a little vinegar has been added and let drain on a towel. This makes the jars shine. Relabel each jar with fancy tags.

To dress up jars that will be presented singly, you can place a circle of calico or gingham, over the top of the jar before putting on the metal ring. Or you can cut a circle from parchment paper and write the name in calligraphy. Attach this paper cover around the jar with a colored elastic.

Apple Butter

It's easy to be put off by old recipes for apple butter. Just reading the part about stirring constantly in an iron kettle over a slow fire all day prompts one to move on! Fortunately, the method can be adapted to the modern kitchen.

*5 pounds tart apples, quartered, with
    blossoms removed*
2 cups apple cider
Sugar
Cloves
Cinnamon

Simmer apples with about an inch of water over low heat until the apples soften. Mash them down as they cook.

Put them through a food mill and measure the pulp. Meanwhile, boil 2 cups of apple cider down to less than 1 cup. Add cider to the pulp along with ½ cup of sugar for each cup of pulp. Add cinnamon and cloves to taste—about ½ teaspoon combined for each 2 cups of pulp. Bring to a boil and cook uncovered over very low heat until most of the liquid has evaporated. Stir frequently, since it sticks very easily.

When there is very little juice left, transfer to a flat glass or pottery baking dish and bake uncovered in a 250°F oven, stirring every 15 minutes. In about 3 or 4 hours, the apple butter will be a rich brown and firm enough to stand up on a spoon. Ladle into hot, sterile jars, seal, and process 15 minutes in boiling water.

Makes approximately 5 half-pint jars.

PEACH CHUTNEY

This spiced condiment adds a lively note to pork roast or chicken. Although tropical chutneys are usually made from mangos, firm peaches make an excellent replacement.

5 pounds peaches
½ pound raisins
½ pound dates, chopped
1 lemon, thinly sliced
2 cups vinegar
3 cups sugar
½ cup fresh lemon or lime juice
½ cup candied ginger, chopped

Peel, pit, and chop peaches. Combine all ingredients and cook until thick, stirring often. As the mixture begins to thicken, keep heat at its lowest setting and stir more frequently. Seal in hot jars and process 15 minutes.

Makes approximately 7 half-pint jars.

© Lynn Karlin

SWEET SLICED PICKLES

Among the oldest of the traditional recipes for pickling cucumbers, this is also one of the easiest and everyone's favorite pickle. Make plenty for your own family, too.

2 quarts thinly sliced cucumbers
2 medium onions, sliced
1 garlic clove, sliced thin
¼ cup salt
½ cup water
1¼ cups cider vinegar
1½ cups sugar
½ teaspoon turmeric
½ teaspoon celery seed
1 tablespoon mustard seed

Combine cucumber, onion, garlic, and salt, and cover with crushed ice. Stir occasionally for 3 hours. Drain and rinse well.

Combine remaining ingredients, except for the water, add to the cucumbers, bring to a boil, and boil 5 minutes. Add the water if there is not enough juice to cover the vegetables. Pour pickles into hot, sterilized jars, seal, and process 15 minutes in boiling water.

Makes approximately 4 pints of pickles.

© Lynn Karlin

PETER PIPER'S PICKLED PEPPERS

Although Mother Goose did not record the exact recipe for the famous peck of pickled peppers, they probably tasted very much like these. Use any hot pepper: jalapeño, cherry, Italian, or other varieties. Red peppers look more festive (and fiery), but green ones taste just as good.

Hot peppers
Cider vinegar
Garlic cloves, peeled

Wash peppers well and pierce in several places with the tip of a knife. Pack peppers as snugly as possible in hot jars, adding a clove of garlic to each. Bring vinegar to a boil and fill jars. Seal and process 15 minutes in boiling water.

© Steven Mark Needham/Envision

OLD-FASHIONED PICCALILLI

A favorite with hotdogs and hamburgers, this relish is equally at home with roast beef or lamb.

6 green tomatoes
4 green peppers
2 sweet red peppers
1 hot pepper
5 onions
¼ cup salt
2½ cups brown sugar
1 teaspoon celery seed
1 tablespoon mustard seed
1 teaspoon whole cloves
1 tablespoon whole allspice
1¾ cups cider vinegar

Slice all vegetables very thin, toss with salt, and leave overnight. Rinse in cold water and drain well. Combine in a large pot with salt, sugar, spices, and vinegar. Bring to a boil and simmer 15 minutes. Seal in hot jars and process for 15 minutes in boiling water.

Makes approximately 4 pints.

Chapter Three

SWEETS

One of the beauties of candy is that it can be made well in advance and stored in sealed tins. You can make it several weeks ahead, perhaps one variety each week, until you have a collection of several ready to package.

Purchase folding candy boxes in various sizes from a candy supply shop and fill with assorted sweets, each in its own separate fluted paper cup. You can buy these cups at any candy supplier, in the housewares section of a department store, or a gourmet shop. They come in red and green holiday designs as well as plain colors. By placing each candy in a cup, you not only protect and separate them, but you make them look even more tempting.

For those who prefer not to eat a lot of candy, use two or three pieces as garnish for a basket or box of other food gifts. If you are shipping a gift to someone in a hot climate, it is best to leave out chocolate-coated candies, since the chocolate is likely to melt before the package is delivered.

PERFECT CHOCOLATE FUDGE

The addition of bitter chocolate to this recipe gives the fudge a rich, dark flavor, while the marshmallow cream provides a velvety texture. Together they make a confection that is unforgettable.

4½ cups of sugar
Pinch of salt
2 tablespoons butter
1 large can of evaporated milk
12 ounces semi-sweet chocolate morsels
8 ounces bitter chocolate, cut fine
2 cups marshmallow cream
2 cups chopped walnut meats

Combine the sugar, salt, butter, and evaporated milk in a heavy saucepan or cast-iron frying pan. Stir and bring to a full rolling boil. Boil hard for exactly 6 minutes.

In a large bowl combine the chocolates, marshmallow, and nuts. Pour the boiling syrup over these and stir until the chocolate has melted completely. There should be no streaks or lumps of chocolate. Pour into two lightly buttered 9 x 9-inch baking pans. Cool several hours, until firm, before cutting into squares.

Makes 4 pounds.

© John and Diane Harper

PEANUT BUTTER FUDGE

Easier than chocolate fudge, but creamy-textured and delicious, this keeps well and packs easily. Package with chocolate fudge to make a checkerboard arrangement.

2 cups sugar
⅔ cup whole milk
1 cup marshmallow cream
1 cup creamy peanut butter
1 teaspoon vanilla

Combine sugar and milk in a saucepan and cook to the soft ball stage (234°F). Stir in marshmallow cream, peanut butter, and vanilla. Stir until the mixture is evenly blended. Pour into a buttered 9-inch square glass baking dish. Allow fudge to stand overnight before cutting into squares.

Makes about 2 pounds.

© John and Diane Harper

© Michael Skott

TURKISH DELIGHT

Gelatin candies can be made in a variety of flavors and sparkling colors using this basic recipe, but none rivals the original Turkish Delight for its delicate rose flavor. These candies may be packed in single layers, but are more elegant if presented in an individual fluted paper candy cup.

½ cup water
2 cups sugar
2½ tablespoons gelatin
½ cup cold water
¼ cup lemon juice
Grated outer rind of one lemon
¼ cup rosewater
1 drop of red food coloring
Confectioner's sugar
¼ cup firmly chopped walnuts
(optional)

Cook ½ cup water with sugar to 255°F and remove from heat. Soften gelatin in ½ cup cold water for 5 minutes. Add to the hot syrup and stir to dissolve completely. Add lemon juice with the grated lemon rind, along with rosewater and food coloring. Stir and pour into a buttered 8-inch square pan. Let stand until quite firm. Cut into cubes and roll in confectioner's sugar.

Makes 64 1-inch squares.

PECAN TURTLES

These rounded mounds of chocolate-covered caramel look like the shells of turtles, while the pecans resemble their feet, hence the name for these old favorites. They are as easy to make as they are to eat.

Light caramel candy squares
Milk chocolate for dipping (Baking
  chocolate may be used, but it is best
  to use chocolate that is specifically
  for dipping.)
Perfect pecan halves

Melt the caramels over hot water in a double boiler. While the candy is melting, arrange pecans on waxed paper in sets of five, radiating from a central point like the points of a star. Pour a spoonful of caramel over the center of each set. Add more caramel if necessary to cover the center half of all the pecans.

While the caramel is setting, melt the chocolate over hot (not boiling) water in a double boiler. The water should not touch the bottom of the chocolate pan. Carefully spoon melted chocolate over the caramel to cover it, but not the tips of the pecan "feet." Allow candies to set overnight before packaging.

HALF-DIPPED APRICOTS

This easy confection is best made with dipping chocolate, which melts to the right consistency and hardens to a lovely gloss without developing white spots. It is found in candy supply shops and some cookware departments.

Perfect, whole, dried apricots
Semisweet chocolate for dipping
    (Baking chocolate may be used, but
    it is best to use chocolate that is
    specifically for dipping.)

Melt the chocolate over hot, not boiling, water in a double boiler. The water should not touch the bottom of the chocolate pan. Carefully dip each apricot into the chocolate so that half of it is submerged, then remove them and place on waxed paper to dry. When they have hardened, package them in individual fluted cups. Muffin cups will do if you cannot find the right size candy cups.

Chapter Four

GIFTS FOR THE COOK

Just because someone is a good cook and enjoys making gifts for others in their own kitchen, does not mean that you should forget them when you are cooking in yours! A particularly welcome gift for the cook would be a special sauce, seasoning blend, or ready-made food that can be used to enhance their own cooking.

If you have an herb garden, package blends of your own dried herbs, or pot chives for their windowsill. If you do not grow herbs, purchase whole spices from a natural food store where they are sold in bulk, and blend these into tempting combinations to flavor hot drinks. Some of the recipes that follow require no cooking at all; the only utensils needed are a bowl and small plastic bags.

These treasures for the cook are at their most elegant when grouped into a basket or small wooden crate or, for a particularly fine gift, into a cooking utensil. Imagine the delight on the face of a friend who receives a collection of your herb or spice blends and condiments packaged in a nonstick wok! Look around in gourmet shops for other container ideas.

BERMUDA HOT SAUCE

Tradition has it that this Bermuda favorite originated when a ship's cook tried to find a way to preserve the hot peppers of the islands for the long voyage home. He put them in sherry and thus was born the famous sauce for steaks, soups, and Bloody Marys. Bottle this in small jars with narrow tops.

Thin, red, hot peppers,
*   fresh or dried*
Sherry

Put one large pepper or several small peppers into each jar and fill with sherry. Cover the jars and store in a dark place for at least a month.

SHERRY-CHEDDAR SPREAD

There is no trick to making this quick gift, except to add the sherry a little at a time to avoid making too runny a spread. If it is too thin, add more cheddar to thicken the mixture. Although a jar makes a perfectly adequate container, the cheese looks more at home in a crock or small pottery bowl covered with plastic wrap.

½ pound well-aged sharp cheddar
cheese
Good sherry wine

Shred cheese and place in blender with ¼ cup sherry. Blend until smooth, adding more wine if necessary to make a smooth spread. Cheese should be stored in the refrigerator and brought out to soften at least an hour before serving.

You can vary this recipe by using different dessert wines, or by adding chopped pecans, walnuts, green olives, or crisp bacon. Team this with a box of Italian breadsticks or plain small crackers, sure to please a busy hostess during the holidays.

Makes approximately 1¼ cups
of spread.

© John and Diane Harper

HERB FETTUCCINE

Even the cook who makes pasta will welcome this delicately flavored herb variety. Fresh herbs, whirred in the blender with the olive oil make a green pasta, but crumbled dried herbs flavor the pasta just as well. If you are using fresh herbs, use one tablespoon of each. Package the fettuccine in a long plastic bag tied with a brightly colored ribbon.

1½ cups flour
1 egg
1 egg white
1 tablespoon olive oil
½ teaspoon basil
½ teaspoon oregano
1 teaspoon salt
A few drops of water

Combine all ingredients except water in a large bowl and knead with fingers to form a dough. Add water to gather the crumbly pieces and knead dough well until it is smooth and elastic. Wrap in waxed paper and allow to stand 15 minutes. If you have a pasta machine, you can use it to roll the dough. Otherwise use a rolling pin and roll one-quarter of the dough at a time, as thin as possible. Cut into ¼-inch-wide strips and hang over a rack or suspended dowel until crisp and dry.

Makes approximately ½ pound of dry pasta.

© Glenn David Smith

HERB BLENDS FOR COOKING

Herbs lend subtle flavoring to many dishes. Although most people use them in such foods as tomato sauce, there are many herb combinations that are less common. Try packaging blends of dried herbs with some small utensil such as a wooden spoon, a wire whisk, or a rubber spatula.

As with teas, the proportion is a matter of taste, so feel free to experiment and create your own combinations. Label each with a list of the foods it goes best with, using the following ideas:

For lamb: rosemary, thyme, and marjoram with dried garlic chips.

For beef: marjoram, thyme, crushed dried red pepper, bay leaf, and savory.

For chicken: savory, basil, rosemary, celery leaves, and peppercorns, with or without garlic chips.

For chicken: tarragon with dried, ground lemon peel.

For Italian sauces: basil, marjoram, oregano, crushed red pepper, and garlic chips.

For Greek salads: spearmint, marjoram, and oregano.

For pork: rosemary, savory, and thyme with garlic chips.

© Burke/Triolo

Steven Mark Needham/Envision

HERB AND FRUIT VINEGARS

You don't have to grow herbs in your backyard to be able to make these tempting additions for salads and sauces. Fresh herbs are available at farmers' markets and grocery stores, or use fresh or frozen fruit to create some of these combinations.

To make any fruit or herb vinegar, wash and sterilize the bottles in boiling water. For herb vinegars, fill the jar one-third full of loosely packed fresh herb sprigs (the leaves should be on the stems) and fill the jar to the top with vinegar. Seal and store for at least two weeks to allow the flavors to blend. For fruit vinegars, fill the jar one-quarter full of fruit and juice, then fill with vinegar.

Different vinegars bring out the best in different herbs. The following list describes some good combinations.

Lemon balm in white distilled vinegar.

Tarragon in white wine vinegar.

Mint in cider vinegar.

Chive blossoms in white distilled vinegar.

Marjoram or basil in red wine vinegar.

Nasturtium blossoms and a garlic clove in white distilled vinegar.

Purple basil in white distilled vinegar.

Fruit vinegars are best made with white distilled vinegar, since it has a mellower flavor and will not interfere with the strong fruit flavors. Try these combinations:

Raspberries with a little white wine;

Lime slices with a clove of garlic;

Cranberries, cranberry juice, and a bay leaf;

Blueberries with a stick of cinnamon.

HERBED MUSTARD

When you are in a hurry for a distinctive condiment to add to your goodie basket, nothing beats this mustard. Present it in the smallest jars you can find, the fancier the better, so they can go right to the table.

A large jar of Dijon-style mustard
Dried dill or tarragon
Freshly ground black pepper
Pinch of ground coriander

© Steven Mark Needham/Envision

Pour mustard into a mixing bowl and add herbs and spices. Use enough herbs so that they will show—this is no time to be stingy. Mix well with a wire whisk and spoon into little jars. Label with the suggestion that the mustard will keep its flavor better if stored in the refrigerator.

Another variation of this theme is to add grated horseradish, well drained, to commercial brown mustard.

VANILLA SUGAR

Anyone who bakes cakes or cookies will delight in this old-fashioned flavored sugar. Make extra for yourself. Present this sugar with the vanilla bean still in it.

Vanilla beans
Granulated sugar

Place a vanilla bean in a jar and fill the jar with sugar. Seal and store at least two weeks before using. Tall apothecary jars make elegant containers for vanilla sugar.

For an even more unusual gift, add a long curl of orange peel that has been removed with a potato peeler and allowed to dry overnight. If you add the peel fresh, the moisture will cause the sugar to cake.

Let the recipient of the sugar know that the bean can be reused—just refill the jar with sugar.

© Steven Mark Needham/Envision

HOT MULLED CIDER SPICES

These are handiest if packaged in small amounts—enough for 4 cups of cider.

1 teaspoon whole cloves
1 teaspoon whole allspice
1 teaspoon broken cinnamon stick
1 teaspoon dried orange peel
1 clove star anise, broken

Combine all ingredients.

Include the following instructions with each packet: Simmer spices in 5 cups of fresh cider for 5 minutes. Strain into cups and top each with a cinnamon stick stirrer.

Makes 4 mugs.

HOT COCOA MIX

Little packets of your own blend of spices, cocoa, and sugar will be appreciated all through the winter. Package each with a cinnamon stick to use as a stirrer.

For each packet you will need:

3 tablespoons dark cocoa powder
2 tablespoons superfine sugar
3 whole cloves
Pinch of ground cinnamon

Mix together all ingredients in a small plastic bag. Or multiply this recipe and present the cocoa mix in a china mug with a bundle of cinnamon sticks tied to the handle. If you do multiply this recipe, place instructions with it saying: To make one cup of cocoa, use 3 heaping tablespoons of mix.

Makes enough for 1 mug of cocoa.

© Michael Kingsford/Envision

TEA BLENDS

China teas flavored with herbs and spices or dried fruits and peels are not only delicious to drink, but easy to make. Since these are loose teas, combine them as a gift with a tea infuser. These have a little perforated "cage" on the end, or are little wicker "baskets" to contain the tea so it can be steeped right in the cup.

Mix the tea and flavorings in a bowl or directly in plastic sandwich bags. There is no magic to the amounts, but a good rule of thumb is to use three parts tea to one part flavorings. All fruit peels should be crisp-dry.

Black tea with peppermint, apple mint, and spearmint leaves.

Black tea with lemon peel and spearmint leaves.

Green tea with jasmine blossoms and lemon peel.

Black tea with cloves, broken cinnamon stick, and orange peel.

Green tea with lemon grass and coriander seeds.

Black tea with spearmint and orange peel with a few whole cloves.

Orange pekoe tea with orange peel, whole cloves, and lemon peel.

HERB TEAS

For those people who prefer herbal teas, you can blend dried herbs into delicate combinations. The quantities and proportions are a matter of taste. Since any one of these herbs can be used alone as a tea, there is no "wrong" herb to have as the predominant one.

Chamomile blossoms alone or with lemon balm or lemon grass.

Rose hips with hibiscus, orange peel, peppermint, and a few cloves.

Peppermint with lemon balm and lemon peel.

Spearmint alone or with lemon peel.

Bergamot (beebalm) leaves alone or with lemon grass.

Chapter Five

~~~~~

KITCHEN CRAFTS

Not every gift that originates in the kitchen is something to eat. A number of fragrant gifts for the house, and some edible gifts for the cook, involve no cooking at all. They are really crafts, but the materials are more likely to be in the kitchen. A spicy pomander to scent any room or a blend of spices to simmer on the back burner as a room freshener use materials right from your spice shelf. Bright strings of dried red peppers, even little wreaths decorated with cinnamon sticks are easy to create right at your own kitchen table.

These gifts keep well and can be made ahead of time.

© Dan Wilby

ONION, SHALLOT, AND GARLIC BRAIDS

The purpose in hanging onions and garlic is not to dry them, but to store them in an airy place where they will keep well.

The long stalks of onion, garlic, and shallot provide a way to braid them into strings. If you cannot get these vegetables fresh from a farm you may have to use the second method in order to string them.

Method #1:

When the tops are dry but not brittle, tie six of them together and begin braid-ing. Add more onions as there is room. When the string is long enough, tie the braid and cut off the remaining ends.

Method #2:

To string onions, shallots, or garlic without long tops, use jute wrapping string or heavy raffia. Make a hanging loop at one end, then tie the twine or raffia firmly around the stem of each bulb. Keep the bulbs close together to form a neat, com-pact string.

RED PEPPER STRINGS

Hot peppers such as the red Italian variety can be strung on long threads to dry, or you can braid jute cord tightly, slipping pepper stems into the braid as you work. Hang these in a dry place that has good air circulation. While the pepper string alone makes a wonderful gift to decorate the kitchen and enliven any cuisine, this could also be presented with a favorite chili recipe.

SPICE BRAID

Although the spices and seasonings on this braid are perfectly good to use, most people will prefer to use this as a decoration for their kitchen. You can use other spices, add dried flowers, or tuck in little bunches of dried herbs.

About 35 strands of raffia, each 24 inches long
A cinnamon stick
24 inches of narrow green or gold ribbon
Whole bay leaves
Small dried red chili peppers
Cinnamon sticks
A small head of garlic or a small cluster of shallots

Fold the raffia bundle in half over the cinnamon stick and divide it into three equal parts. Braid the raffia and tie it at the bottom, leaving about 3 inches unbraided at the bottom. Tie the garlic or shallots over the tie, or stick the stem through the tie to secure it over the braid. Carefully push chili peppers into the braid in a starburst shape around the garlic. Above these, push bay leaves into the braid, which will form an attractive arrangement. Break cinnamon sticks lengthwise to make very narrow ones and push these into the braid.

Tie each end of the ribbon to an end of the cinnamon stick at the top to form a hanger, as you would hang a scroll.

SPICE SACHETS

Pile bundles of these sachets in a basket or fill an apothecary jar with them. Use them individually in place of bows on packages and as a "garnish" in gift baskets.

4 squares of calico or gingham fabric, 6 inches square and cut with pinking scissors
4 matching or contrasting narrow ribbons, each 12 inches long
1 tablespoon whole cloves
1 tablespoon whole allspice
1 tablespoon broken stick cinnamon
1 tablespoon dried orange peel

Lay a square of fabric on your work surface, right side down. Place a tablespoonful of the mixed spices and the peel in the center and bring the centers of all four sides together over the spices. This will leave the corners standing out. With the other hand, gather the corners into the center, just above the pile of spices, to make a firm, round bundle. Tie with the ribbon, making a neat bow. Pull the corners of the fabric so they stand out. Repeat with the other squares.

Makes 4 sachets.

POMANDER

Although many "recipes" for pomanders suggest rolling them in powdered orris root and ground spices after they are finished, this is unnecessary. They will remain fragrant for years without this unsightly coating. They not only look better, but they are not irritating to the many people who are allergic to orris.

Begin with firm fruit of any size. Push the stems of whole cloves into the surface of the fruit so their edges just barely touch. The fruit will shrink as it dries, so there has to be some space between the cloves. Leave the indentations around the stem and blossom, since they will recede into the fruit as the pomander dries. Place the pomander in a dry place with good air circulation. Each day, roll it very gently in your palms to push the cloves into the drying fruit. When the fruit is partly dry, push a bent wire or a hairpin into the stem end to form a hanging loop. When the pomander is thoroughly dry, tie a bow to the loop.

© Michael Skott

SOURCES

Herbitage Farm
686 Old Homestead
Highway
Richmond, NH 03470
*Pomander and sachet kits,
cinnamon sticks (catalog
$1.00)*

Aphrodisia
282 Bleecker Street
New York, NY 10014
*Dried herbs and spices,
vanilla beans (informative
catalog $2.00)*

INDEX